20 TH CENTURY

fashion

THE 20s & 30s

FLAPPERS & VAMPS

20TH CENTURY FASHION – THE '20s & '30s
was produced by

David West ﷽ **Children's Books**
7 Princeton Court
55 Felsham Road
London SW15 1AZ

Picture Research: Carlotta Cooper/Brooks Krikler
Research
Editor: Clare Oliver
Consultant: Helen Reynolds

First published in Great Britain in 1999 by
Heinemann Library, Halley Court, Jordan Hill,
Oxford OX2 8EJ, a division of Reed Educational and
Professional Publishing Limited.

OXFORD MELBOURNE AUCKLAND
JOHANNESBURG BLANTYRE GABORONE
IBADAN PORTSMOUTH (NH) USA CHICAGO

01 00 99
10 9 8 7 6 5 4 3 2 1

ISBN 0 431 09549 3 (HB)
ISBN 0 431 09556 6 (PB)

British Library Cataloguing in Publication Data

Blackman, Cally
Flappers and vamps (1920s - 1930s). - (Fashion in the
twentieth century)
1. Fashion - History - 20th century - Juvenile
literature
2. Costume - 20th century - Juvenile literature
I. Title
391'.00904

Printed and bound in Italy.

PHOTO CREDITS :
Abbreviations: t-top, m-middle,
b-bottom, r-right, l-left
Cover tl, bl & pages 3tl, 4b, 8-9, 12-
13b, 22tl, 22-23, 23tr, 23l, 25br:
Kobal Collection; Cover tr, m &
pages 3tr, 4t, 5ml, 6bl, 7br, 8tr, 8b,
11tl, 11tr, 12tl, 13br, 14bl, 15tl, 16b,
17br, 18tl, 18b, 19tr, 19br, 22mr,
24bl: Mary Evans Picture Library;
Cover ml & page 6t: H. Meserdle ©
Vogue/Condé Nast Publications Ltd;
Cover mr, br & pages 3br, 7bl, 27bl:
Beaton © Vogue/Condé Nast
Publications Ltd; Cover bm & pages
5t, 10tr, 12bl, 14t, 15tr, 16tr, 20tl,
20tr, 20br, 21tl, 21tr, 21bl, 26m:
Vogue Magazine © Vogue/Condé
Nast Publications Ltd; 5br: Studio
Sun © Vogue/Condé Nast
Publications Ltd; 6br, 8tl, 9t, 9b, 12-
13t, 14-15, 15br, 18-19, 19bl, 24-25,
25tr, 26tl, 29tl, 29br: Hulton Getty;
7t, 11bl: Steichen © Vogue/Condé
Nast Publications Ltd; 10tl, 17ml:
Bruehl-Bourges © Vogue/Condé Nast
Publications Ltd; 10b: Helen Dryden
© Vogue/Condé Nast Publications
Ltd; 11br: George Plank ©
Vogue/Condé Nast Publications Ltd;
13mr: Douglas Pollard ©
Vogue/Condé Nast Publications Ltd;
16tl: Georges Lapape ©
Vogue/Condé Nast Publications Ltd;
17tr: Hoyningen-Huene ©
Vogue/Condé Nast Publications Ltd;
21br, 23br, 29m: Corbis; 24tl: Scotts
© Vogue/Condé Nast Publications
Ltd; 26br: Carl Erickson ©
Vogue/Condé Nast Publications Ltd;
27tl, 28: Schenker © Vogue/Condé
Nast Publications Ltd; 27br: Vogue
Studio © Vogue/Condé Nast
Publications Ltd.

With special thanks to the Picture
Library & Syndication Department
at Vogue Magazine/Condé Nast
Publications Ltd.

*An explanation of difficult
words can be found in the
glossary on page 30.*

20TH CENTURY fashion

THE 20s & 30s

FLAPPERS & VAMPS

Cally Blackman

Heinemann LIBRARY

CONTENTS

The '20s saw some wild dance crazes, such as the charleston, advertized here at the Folies-Bergère cabaret in Paris.

Gang warfare in the United States inspired a string of gangster films, many starring James Cagney. The first was The Public Enemy ('31).

Between the WARS

After the horrors of World War I, there was a general feeling of freedom in the early 1920s. Women who had worked during the war found a new financial and social independence. The social scene was dominated by vamps and flappers – boyish, youthful women who wore skimpy dresses, make-up, and smoked in public.

But this gaiety was shortlived. Many European countries were left with large war debts and these, along with rising inflation and disasters on the stock markets, led to the worst recession of the 20th century. There was political turmoil in Europe: fascism and communism fought it out in a bloody civil war in Spain (1936–39). This war inspired Spanish painter Pablo Picasso's masterpiece *Guernica* ('37).

In the United States, Prohibition was introduced: far from putting an end to alcohol, it created a black market controlled by the gangsters of the day. The most famous, Al Capone, was said to be worth $100 million in 1927.

As always, fashion was influenced by the events around it. As the depression took hold, wild flapper dresses gave way to sober but feminine fashions.

Cinema was the chief form of entertainment and 'talkies' came in with *The Jazz Singer* (1927). Hollywood led the styles for flappers, vamps and then '30s elegance: Macy's in New York sold 500,000 copies of an evening gown worn by Joan Crawford.

With the outbreak of World War II in 1939, the silver screen was to be the only source of glamour and escapism for several years to come.

Flappers wore drop-waisted dresses stitched with pearls, crystals and tiny mirrors ('25). Hair cuts were short and boyish.

Shopping became a hobby: happy shoppers travelled off-peak to the big department stores and came home laden with parcels. Even working in a department store was glamorous: film star Greta Garbo was 'discovered' as a shop girl in Stockholm!

By the '30s, the chief item of daywear was the suit and hemlines dropped back below the knee. Sensible styles reflected the economic worries of the time.

GIRLS *will be* BOYS

During World War I many women had worked for the first time. Afterwards, this new financial independence and greater equality enabled women to pursue a freer lifestyle. By 1928 all women over 21 in Britain could vote: sex barriers were gradually broken down.

This Vogue *cover ('24) showed the fashion for costume jewellery. Beads were worn long and sometimes knotted.*

SIMPLY SHORT

Women's dress reflected this new liberation: fashion became more practical as women now led more active lives. The fussiness of the Edwardian era disappeared – clothes were shaped like simple tubes with dropped waistlines and skirts became shorter. The main garments were longish coats worn over either a dress or a long blouse and a skirt. It was very fashionable for the coat lining to match the dress underneath. Suits were also worn during the day, made of wool or tweed, often belted at the waist. The wealthy sometimes wore them with fur collars.

FLATTER FIGURES

The emphasis was on youth and a slim, boyish body. Restrictive corsets were replaced by cylindrical underwear that flattened the chest and had attached suspenders to hold up stockings. Underwear was much simpler and some young people dispensed with petticoats.

Before '24 stockings were made of dark wool or cotton. With the invention of rayon came 'nude' stockings that showed off the legs.

COCO CHANEL

Chanel was probably the most influential designer of the '20s. Her elegant clothes inspired the *garçonne* (French for 'boy') look. She made cardigan suits, sailor jackets, pullovers and trousers in soft, jersey fabrics. These were worn with costume jewellery. She was one of the first to open a boutique (in Biarritz).

In '21 Coco Chanel (below, in a cardigan suit) launched her 'Chanel No 5' perfume. Five was her lucky number.

COLOURS OF FASHION

Neutral colours such as beige were common. This was sometimes called 'the ghost of khaki' as so much of this dye was left over after the war. However, the influence of the Russian Ballet brought in brighter colours such as purples and oranges, particularly for eveningwear.

Chanel's easy-to-wear clothes ('26) included drop-waisted jersey dresses (left) or silk skirts worn with a jersey sweater and a cardigan (right).

Hats were always worn outside during the day. Most fashionable was the cloche (French for 'bell'), as worn by this Vogue cover girl ('24).

BOYISH BOBS

Women had begun to cut their hair during the war to avoid accidents in factories. By the early 1920s everyone was wearing the fashionable bob, then the shingle (slightly waved). These styles were followed by the even more boyish Eton crop.

FAB FOOTWEAR

Shoes had low, Cuban or louis (hourglass-shaped) heels with a strap across the instep. Evening shoes were often decorated with a buckle rather like those worn by men in the 1700s. Russian boots were popular when skirts were at their shortest.

CHEAP CHIC

Inexpensive ready-made clothing became available in stores such as the 'Co-op', or Burton's for menswear, which provided fashions at affordable prices. It was easy to follow fashion as many new womens' magazines and journals were produced. Home dress-making became popular, with magazines featuring patterns for sewing, knitwear and crochet.

Sewing machines were cheap to buy, so many women made their own clothes, including the new, simple styles of underwear.

The GREAT GATSBY

Knickerbockers were worn by both sexes. In the US, a law had to be overturned before women were able to wear them.

In the 1920s, older men still wore Edwardian-style clothes: formal frock coats or morning coats, and tails and white tie for eveningwear. But the younger generation were choosing a more relaxed style.

It was the fashion to spend the week in the town but weekends in the country. Even at the weekend, double-breasted suits and panama hats were worn.

LOUNGING AROUND

Lounge suits, made in softer fabrics such as checked tweeds and grey flannel, were cut more loosely and were more comfortable than before. Shoulders were wider, armholes were bigger, jackets were longer and trousers had more room at the top. Zips started to replace button flies. Soft shirt collars for informal wear replaced stiff, starched ones. Ties could be brightly patterned, but occasionally were not worn at all. Patent shoes were worn with evening dress, while for the day, brogues were usually worn. Some men still wore two-tone spats, but these were gradually worn only at formal occasions, such as weddings.

There was more choice for men than ever before. These fashion plates show the formal, casual and sporty looks worn around '27.

Author F. Scott Fitzgerald was known for his own fast living. His novel The Great Gatsby ('25) documents the wild excesses of the rich during the '20s. The story was made into a film starring Robert Redford as Jay Gatsby ('74).

It was polite to wear a hat when outdoors. Here, artist Cecil Beaton (left) attended the annual Eton-Harrow match ('27) in a 'topper'. For less formal occasions, boaters, Homburgs and panama hats were all popular styles.

BAGGY TROUSERS

In 1925 some fashionable young men at Oxford University began the rage for wearing Oxford bags – baggy flannel trousers which were half a metre wide at the bottom – or more! Adapted from sportswear, these were one of the most outrageous styles of the century.

OFF THE PEG

Those who could afford to, went to a tailor for their suits and London tailoring was considered to be the best in the world. Ready-made suits were becoming increasingly available, although they still tended not to fit very well.

THE DUKE OF WINDSOR

The Duke of Windsor (*right*, in '37) was a key fashion figure. As Prince of Wales he wore generously-cut suits in colourful tweeds, checks or stripes and introduced the 'Windsor knot' for ties. He also started the trend for patterned Fair Isle jumpers in '22.

The Duke of Windsor became, briefly, King Edward VIII of Britain, but he abdicated in '36 so that he could marry an American divorcée, Mrs Wallis Simpson (left).

ART *deco: a total look*

Art deco was the most important design movement of the 1920s and the forerunner of modernism in the '30s. It swept away the graceful and sinuous lines of art nouveau.

Art deco style was mostly seen in interior design, but it influenced all other arts, from fashion to packaging.

DECORATIVE ARTS

Art deco style took its name from an exhibition held in Paris in 1925, called the *Exposition Internationale des* Arts Decoratifs *et Industriels Modernes.* The style was influenced by major artistic movements such as cubism and futurism which celebrated the fast-moving modernisation of the time. These art styles often featured blocks of brilliant flat colours and abstract, angular shapes. Favourite motifs were simple, stylized flowers, fountains, leaping gazelles, sunbursts and lightning zigzags. Ideas for these geometric patterns often came from Aztec and Egyptian art styles.

The influence of Aztec art can be seen in the geometric patterns on the coats worn by these Vogue *cover girls ('25).*

A TOTAL LOOK

All forms of the applied arts were affected by art deco, including textiles, graphics and ceramics. But its greatest impact was in the fields of architecture and interior design: the great temples to art deco include the Chrysler Building and Radio City Music Hall, both in New York. Everything – from the outside decoration to the radiator grilles inside – was part of the look, and great attention was paid to the smallest detail.

A stylized art deco screen and tiled floor provide the perfect backdrop for this elegant outfit ('22).

LES BALLETS RUSSES

The arrival of the Russian Ballet in Paris in 1909 is sometimes seen as the start of art deco. The director, Sergei Diaghilev, used oriental-style costumes in vibrant colours – oranges, yellows, purples, jades and pinks. The look reflected the gaiety of the early '20s and was popularised by French designer Paul Poiret.

Costumes for the Ballets Russes' productions influenced fashion for many years. Those for Midnight Sun (shown left and right), used rich embroidery and appliqué.

Paul Poiret had been admired before the war for his exotic styles. In the '20s, he led the way with minimalist, graphic styles of decoration.

TEXTILES & PATTERNS

Two artists led the field of textiles: Russian-born Sonia Delaunay (1884–1979) and Frenchman Raoul Dufy (1877–1953). Both worked for the textile company Bianchini-Fsérier, which specialized in hand-printed silks. Delaunay's designs often featured circles in bright colours. Dufy's textiles were bold and graphic, too: he would take a simple motif, such as a stylized turtle or vegetable and repeat it to great effect. Dufy worked with designer Paul Poiret (1879–1944) on fabrics for clothes and furnishings.

TONING IT DOWN

At first, the art deco style required lavish tambour embroidery, drawing inspiration from every possible source. But by the mid-1920s a less decorative look came in. Detail was pared down to a few, carefully-placed motifs. Fashionable interior designers favoured white rooms with all-white furnishings instead of colour and patterns, and streamlined chrome and glass gave a modern feel.

In the early days of art deco, decoration was as exotic as possible. Fashion plates took influence from the east ('23).

VAMPS & FLAPPERS

Having survived World War I, young people were determined to enjoy life to the full. Those from wealthy families were sometimes called the Bright Young Things. Their wild social life centred around parties, nightclubs and weekend house parties and their fun-loving antics shocked the older generation.

Young women broke all the old rules by appearing in public without a chaperone.

FAST-LIVING GIRLS

Young women who adopted the new boyish look, danced all night, smoked in public and wore make-up were called vamps or flappers. Women could now go out with friends without a chaperone. Nightclubs were the fashionable place to go and cocktails became popular.

EYE-CATCHING EVENINGWEAR

Evening-dress was the same length as daywear. Simple sheath dresses relied for impact on fabulous fabrics and surface decoration, such as complicated beading.

For a night out on the town an ostrich feather fan was the most fashionable accessory for cooling down. Another essential was a long cigarette holder.

The flapper look was immortalized on the silver screen in the Hollywood film Thoroughly Modern Millie *('67). It starred Julie Andrews as a young girl who goes to New York in the '20s.*

Fancy dress balls, such as this one held in '22, were all the rage. Many costumes took an eastern theme, with exotic beading or risqué belly-dancer outfits. Harlequin or clown suits were other firm favourites.

Another popular decoration was fringing, which moved with the wearer. The emphasis was on the hips – drop-waisted dresses were trimmed with sashes or artificial flowers placed to one side at the waistline. Evening coats which fastened low on the hips were made in rich brocades or velvets and often had fur collars and cuffs.

SHEER STYLE

The nude look – bare arms, neck and legs – was played up by the use of sheer fabrics such as light silks, satins, chiffons, organzas and tulles. Silver or gold lamé gave a fashionable oriental or Arabian feel. Madeleine Vionnet became mistress of the 'bias cut' – cutting fabric diagonally across the grain to achieve a soft, draping effect. Dispensing with the corset her shapes were fluid and simple. By the end of the decade, as skirt lengths went down again, dresses were made to look longer by the use of handkerchief points or uneven hems.

FINISHING TOUCHES

Long strings of beads or pearls suited the flat-fronted dresses, and earrings were worn long. The head was kept small and neat, and a bandeau of fabric, perhaps with a feather in it, was worn. Eyes were rimmed with make-up, and the eyelids were greased to make them shiny. Lips were painted bright red.

THE JAZZ AGE

The Dixieland Jazz Band, formed in '16 in New Orleans, started a craze for jazz – and wild new dances! In '26 the charleston became popular. Performers such as American chorus girl Josephine Baker (1906–75) were the height of fashion.

Dancing at the Folies-Bergère, Paris, Josephine Baker shocked the world with costumes made of a few ostrich feathers or beads – and little else!

Madeleine Vionnet was known for the clever cut of her designs. The pointed hemline of this evening-dress ('26) is emphasized by long silk tassels at the front and back.

SPORTY *styles*

The new popularity of sporting and outdoor activities meant that there was now emphasis on a slim figure for both men and women. The clothing worn for these activities had a tremendous impact on fashion. Amelia Earhart (1898–1937), who flew solo across the Atlantic in '32, even started her own fashion collection.

Skiwear ('26): a waterproofed skirt and jacket, with black-and-white calfskin trim.

FREEDOM TO MOVE

Many casual fashions of the 1920s and '30s started life as sportswear. Sporty clothes were lighter and more comfortable. The Norfolk suit was popular for boys and for everyday wear in the country. Originally worn for shooting, it had two deep pleats in the back of the jacket for ease of movement.

By '34 sporting flannel trousers and tennis shorts featured state-of-the-art elastic waists.

TEE-TIME TWEEDS

Golf was very popular for both sexes. Men wore tweed or flannel plus-fours tucked into patterned socks, while women wore pleated, gored tweed skirts. Both sexes wore patterned jumpers or plain cardigans. Long thin scarves and cloche hats were also worn for golf.

ANYONE FOR TENNIS?

Sports stars became as glamorous as film stars and influenced fashion. Until the appearance of French tennis star Suzanne Lenglen (1899–1938), women had worn everyday clothes for tennis.

Plus-fours were worn for playing golf. True plus-fours hung four inches (10cm) below the knee; the shorter plus-twos finished two inches (5cm) below the knee.

Lenglen dressed in practical, short (calf-length), pleated tennis skirts and sleeveless dresses. She also appeared on court without stockings, which was considered very shocking. In 1933 Alice Marble (1913–90) caused a sensation when she appeared at Wimbledon wearing shorts!

Lenglen's tennis wardrobe was created by French designer Jean Patou.

LE SKI

Women, who competed in the Olympics from 1928, took part in competitive skiing. During the '30s, it grew very popular. Elsa Schiaparelli (1890–1973) designed transparent oilskins and tortoise-shell goggles. Ski suits were made in waterproofed gabardine, silk, wool, jersey or cord. Cuffs were tight-fitting, thanks to the new Lastex yarn, while zips made garments more practical.

For some activities, such as sailing, trousers were the only sensible option for women to wear by '36.

SPORTS & SHORTS

The fashion for slimness also promoted keep-fit routines and squash. Cycling and hiking were favourite pastimes, and women wore shorts for these activities. Trousers were worn by women on the beach and as leisurewear.

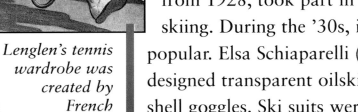

SPORTY KNITS

Until the '20s, knitwear was worn only as underwear or for sports. Polo neck jumpers were first worn by polo players; V-necks by cricketers; and sweaters were worn by 19th-century health fanatics who exercised dressed in wool. From the early '20s there was a vogue for bright, patterned jumpers. Patterned Fair Isle knits came in after the Duke of Windsor wore one on the golf course.

By the mid-'30s, knitwear designs were chic and monochrome.

Sun & sand

Before the war, a suntan was a sign of being an outdoor labourer, but in the 1920s the rich and fashionable began to strip off on the beach. Sunbathing was thought to be good for you, and was part of the new quest for healthy outdoor pursuits.

Many more people had access to motor cars. Jaunts to the seaside in a sporty, open-top car were very popular.

Patou created these silk bathing shoes ('27) and the black-and-white bathing suit (right); two-tone suits, such as this one (left) were also in vogue.

SUN WORSHIP

Resorts such as the French Riviera, Biarritz and Le Touquet in France, and California and Miami in the United States became the smart places for the wealthy to go on holiday. Chanel, one of the first to wear a tan, had opened a boutique in Biarritz in 1915 to cater for her rich clientèle. The middle and working classes also enjoyed seaside holidays: holiday camps, such as Butlins, sprang up. Near-nudity was no longer taboo, and men and women enjoyed the sea and sun together.

Ocean liners were lavish, floating hotels. Cruises required a huge wardrobe: full evening-dress for dinner dances and sunbathing outfits for lounging around the on-deck pool.

SKIMPY SWIMWEAR

Womens' bathing costumes – which before had been almost like dresses with bloomers – got skimpier: the idea was to expose as much skin to the sun as possible. They could consist of a tunic-shaped top over long knickers, a one-piece costume, or, by the early-1930s, a daring two-piece – forerunner of the bikini. They were made in cotton, wool, or silk jersey fabrics or hand-knitted in wool. These knitted costumes tended to sag or shrink, and soon manufacturers began to produce non-shrink, non-stretch yarn which kept its shape, and supplied patterns to go with it. Many womens' magazines of the day included knitting patterns for bathing costumes.

MACHO TRUNKS

Men, who had previously worn all-in-one bathing costumes when ladies were present, began to wear topless trunks in the mid-1920s. Before this trunks had only been worn in competitions. These usually had a belt at the waist. Both men and women wore rubber bathing caps.

BEACH ACCESSORIES

Now costumes were skimpier, more clothes were required for lounging on the beach. Towelling wraps and beach pyjamas with wide legs were popular, as well as halter-neck tops worn with shorts. Now that people wanted a tan, painted parasols became less necessary. People wore floppy straw or fabric hats to shade out the sun and, during the 1930s, the hats came off, and sunglasses became fashionable. To protect the feet, strappy sandals, espadrilles or canvas shoes were worn.

Holiday attire for the wealthy tourists in Biarritz included pleated wool and jersey skirts and cloche hats.

Beach fashions, '34: the straw hat shades the eyes from the glare of the sun, while strappy espadrilles protect the feet from the burning sand.

SKIN CARE

Jean Patou brought out 'Chaldee' in '27 – the first suntan oil. Ambre Solaire was another early suncare product and remains the leading brand. Ordinary make-up, too, had to take account of the new sun-kissed complexion. Max Factor introduced his colour harmony approach and sold powders, lipsticks and blusher that matched the wearer's skin.

By the '30s, there was a big range of holiday cosmetics, including 'Zon', which promised to make the wearer 'a glorious brown'.

ZON SUN BATHING OIL
MAKES YOU A GLORIOUS BROWN

Prevents SUNBURN BLISTERING & IS ANTI-MIDGE BITE

1'6 & 2'9

The GREAT DEPRESSION

The endless parties were enjoyed by a wealthy few. Most people were suffering the century's most serious economic crisis, the Great Depression. Unemployment was high. Trade unions and political movements struggled for more power.

The General Strike of May '26 caused total chaos.

SOCIAL CONDITIONS

After the war, the gulf between the 'haves' and 'have-nots' widened. Housing conditions, health care and education were poor. Although working-class communities were close-knit and supportive, many people were on the breadline. In 1926 in Britain a General Strike was called in support of the miners. The country came to a standstill for nine days. During the strike, some young socialites drove ambulances, buses and trams, thinking that it was rather fun, but by the end of the '20s, those same people had more sympathy for the workers.

Settlers went to the Mid-West of the United States in search of a new life. Swirling storms of dust destroyed any chance of this.

In '32 there were breadlines in Sixth Avenue and 42nd Street, New York City when poor people queued up for handouts of free food.

STOCK MARKET CRASH

The 1929 Wall Street Crash caused a devastating economic depression, first in the United States and then all over Europe. Billions of dollars worth of shares were wiped out in less than a week of frantic selling on the New York stock exchange. Many speculators lost their life savings – some even committed suicide.

In '36, unemployed people marched on London from Jarrow in northern England. Many were nearly starving. The hunger marchers made people aware of how unfair society was.

DUST TO DUST

During the 1930s unemployment spiralled. As more workers were laid off, fewer people could afford to buy goods, so even more workers lost their jobs. In the United States, several years of drought combined with over-farming in the Mid-West created a 'Dustbowl' where nothing could grow. By digging up the prairies, the farmers had lost the soil's natural protection from the winds. People lost everything and moved back to the cities, but there was no work there, either.

A historic moment: Italian leader Benito Mussolini visited the German leader Adolf Hitler in '37.

LA TRIBUNA ILLUSTRATA

Supplemento illustrato de "La Tribuna"

LA STORICA VISITA DEL DUCE AL FÜHRER
I due Condottieri acclamati dal grande popolo tedesco

RIGHT-WING IDEAS ...

In Europe, extreme political movements emerged. Fascist leaders came to power, promising to restore national pride and create jobs: Benito Mussolini (1883–1945) took over in Italy in '22; Austrian-born Adolf Hitler (1889–1945) came to power in Germany in '33 and Francisco Franco (1892–1975) ruled Spain from '36.

... AND LEFT-WING IDEALS

Communism seemed to offer another solution. Its idea of work and shared wealth for all appealed to many people. These social concerns affected fashion. Clothing became more sober in the 1930s, as people did not want to display their wealth in a conspicuous way any more.

WEALTHY EXCESSES

Germany was ripe for change when Hitler came to power. The Kit Kat Klub in Berlin (setting of *Cabaret*, the '72 film starring Liza Minelli) was a hot-bed of vice and excess.

In '30s Germany most people were terribly poor but the rich indulged in expensive clothes and pastimes.

SCREEN *idols*

Cinema became the most popular form of entertainment during the 1920s and '30s. Film stars were idolized, and everyone tried to imitate the look and style of his or her favourite star.

Clara Bow was known as the 'It' girl, after starring in the film It *('27).*

VAMPS OF THE HAREM

The vamp look of the early 1920s was inspired by the silent films – the term came from the vampire movies made at the time. The greatest vamp of all was Theda Bara (1890–1955). Her kohl-rimmed eyes, blood-red lips and exotic outfits in *Cleopatra* ('17) and *Salomé* ('18) remained in vogue into the '20s. Gloria Swanson (1899–1983) was another sensuous star. She appeared in many feature films in the early '20s before setting up her own film company.

FILMS & FLAPPERS

American actresses Louise Brooks (1906–85) and Clara Bow (1905–65) were model flappers: Brooks' glossy bob still looks modern today, while Bow created a trend for painted, cupid's bow lips.

Pin-ups of the age: the glamorous Gloria Swanson with actor Rudolph Valentino.

MOVIE MEN

The leading man of the 1920s was Italian-born Rudolph Valentino (1895–1926). Whether in immaculate dinner suit or a sheikh's robes, he made women faint in admiration: his early death drove some fans to suicide. Cary Grant (1904–1986) always wore fine suits, while Fred Astaire's (1899–1987) outfits ranged from white tie and tails, to open-necked shirts and slacks.

Cary Grant wore suits that padded out his body, so that his head would appear smaller.

Garbo popularized a more masculine look: minimal make-up, elegant knits and chic trouser suits.

GORGEOUS GARBO

Greta Garbo (1905–90) starred in 27 films. Dressed by the American designer Adrian (1903–59), she wore masculine trousers, men's overcoats and berets. For her role in *A Woman of Affairs* ('28), Adrian created a large, pull-down cloche, known as a slouch hat.

COSTUMIERS

Adrian also created bias-cut dresses for sex symbol Jean Harlow (1911–37) and Joan Crawford (1904–86). Costumier Edith Head (1899–1981) created sultry clothes for Mae West (1882–1980) and Marlene Dietrich (1901–1992). Though some fashion designers, including Chanel, designed for the movies, the costumiers understood the industry better and created looks that were not out-of-date by the time the film came out.

HOLLYWOOD HAIRSTYLES

Cinema-goers avidly copied their idols: Jean Harlow dyed her hair platinum blonde and many women copied her, even though the peroxide was painful and ruined the hair.

Even children braved the new 'permanent wave machines' to achieve sleek curls.

Fred Astaire and Ginger Rogers wowed the world with their slick dance routines. From '33 to '49, they starred together in ten musicals.

GANGSTER *suits*

Although London tailoring was still considered to be the best in the world, the influence of Hollywood stars and well-dressed gangster celebrities, meant that by the 1930s the United States led the way in mens' fashions.

Pinstripes were no longer just for men as this smart lady's suit ('36) demonstrates.

ALL SORTS OF SUITS

The suit was made in lighter fabrics and louder patterns such as checks and stripes. It was cut wide at the shoulders, gangster-style, and could be double- or single-breasted with wide, pointed lapels. Trousers were fastened with zip flies instead of button flies and kept up by a belt rather than braces.

A double-breasted overcoat gave men a slimline silhouette ('27), especially when worn with a banded trilby.

The single-breasted suit gave a fuller look. Overcoats were generously cut with wide shoulders. Raglan sleeves made these roomy and more comfortable.

SUMMER STYLES

American style was most apparent in light summer clothing and sportswear. Summer suits were made in fabrics such as crinkly seersucker, shantung (raw silk) and linen. Shorts and open-necked shirts were worn on holiday, and casual slacks were worn for sport with zipped blousons or windcheater-style jackets.

Knitwear was increasingly worn with suits or perhaps under a blazer with flannel trousers. The patterned jumpers of the 1920s gave way to plainer designs in polo neck, cricket and fishing styles. Footwear too, was made more lightweight and comfortable. Styles included suede shoes with crepe soles, loafers, canvas plimsolls and leather sandals.

HATS OFF FOR THE TRILBY

Hats were still usually worn out of doors and always for formal wear. Bowler hats and Homburgs were worn to the office, while the favourite informal hat was the trilby with a silk band. It was worn with the brim snapped down at the front and up at the back. The hair, which had been slicked back with brilliantine during the 1920s was now grown a little longer and softly waved.

TIMES THEY ARE A-CHANGIN'

Wristwatches now replaced fob-watches (which were still worn by more old-fashioned men). They had been developed in the early part of the century so that people could tell the time easily when driving, travelling or playing sport. During the 1930s they were made in stylish rectangular shapes which reflected the sleek modernism of the decade.

Gangster Al Capone (centre) *was arrested in '31.*

GANGSTERS

During Prohibition in the United States ('20–'33), alcohol was illegal and gangs controlled the black market. In '29 rivalry between Chicago gangs led to the St Valentine's Day Massacre. Capone's men shot seven men from a rival gang.

Film star James Cagney popularized the gangster look in The Public Enemy *('31).*

FRONT *to back*

Actress Joan Barry wore this backless gown in The Port *('33). Full, flared sleeves and the bow at the back emphasize the bare expanse of skin.*

In the 1930s, women's eveningwear became much more sophisticated than before. Full-length evening-dresses that plunged at the back were the most tantalizing style of the decade.

BACK OFF

Backless evening-dresses were cut right down to the waist at the back and high at the front. The back of the dress was also the focal point for detailing with drapes, bows and accessories. American-born Mainbocher (1891–1976) used the bias cut to great effect in his gowns and produced short bolero jackets to wear over the top. He was the favourite designer of Mrs Simpson and created her dress when she married the Duke of Windsor.

Molyneux's designs ('36) included a yellow gown whose skirt separated to flash the leg as the wearer walked (right). A generous scarf drapes to show off the nape of the neck and the back (left).

SLINKY & SEXY

The slim, streamlined look was emphasized by the use of slippery satins, fluid crepes, sheer voiles and slinky silks, in solid colours or floral prints. The bias cut gave a hip-hugging silhouette which flared out towards the ankles. These fabrics were sometimes embroidered or overlaid with lace, styles which harked back to the romantic past.

This lamé creation by Lelong ('34) revisits the turn-of-the-century bustle. The dress features a hooded cape, known as a capuchon, which drapes over the back in low folds.

Other features borrowed from the past included bustles that showed off the tightness of the dress on the hip, short trains and elegant fantails, as shown by Schiaparelli.

CHEAPER CLOTH

Although the fuller lines of garments required more fabric than in the 1920s, a response to the economic depression could

FURS
Throughout the '20s and '30s wearing fur was very popular. All kinds of furs were used, including monkey, leopard and ocelot. Fox was especially fashionable, with one or two skins being worn around the shoulders, held together by clips in the foxes' mouths. Women didn't consider where the furs came from – they were just another expression of glamour.

The extravagant ermine evening coat (right) had a fox fur collar.

be seen in the use of cheaper fabrics for the evening. In 1931 Chanel's collection included 35 evening-dresses in different types of cotton: piqué, lace, muslin, organdie, lawn and net. At the bottom end of the market artificial silk, or rayon, was used.

DIAMONDS FOREVER

As in the 1920s, long strands of beads were worn, but now they were slung over the back to draw yet more attention to it. Small studs and clips replaced long dangly earrings; chunky jewellery in geometric shapes looked very modern and showed the influence of art deco. Cartier designed fantastical jewellery at this time, often teaming diamonds with another precious stone, such as emerald or sapphire, to create pieces in the shape of animals. But the economic depression made it bad taste to display wealth and generally accessories were kept simple.

A slim evening gown by Schiaparelli ('34) shows her trademark wit: the stiff fantail highlights the narrow hips above. A shiny, patterned jacket completed the look.

May '38: embroidery (left) and floral prints (right) harked back to the tea gowns worn 30 years earlier. Now, however, these floor-sweeping styles were only for eveningwear.

The TECHNOLOGY *behind the*

The 1920s and '30s saw many new developments in the textile industry. The first artificial fabric, rayon, came into its own and was used widely. The period also saw the production of new elastic yarns and there were important advances in knitting.

THE BIRTH OF RAYON

Rayon is known as an artificial (man-made) fibre but not a synthetic one because it starts out with a natural ingredient – wood pulp or wood chips. The process for making it was discovered in 1892, ending a long search which had begun in the 1600s. The first 'art. silk' (short for artificial silk) plant opened in the United States in 1910 and in '24 the new yarn was given the name rayon.

Rayon's silky feel made it ideal for the slinky gowns of the '30s, such as this one in white satin rayon ('36).

THE RAYON YEARS

Rayon's cheapness made it a popular fabric for those who could not afford real silk. In 1920 when skirt lengths rose, women wanted to wear 'art. silk' stockings which gave a huge boost to the hosiery industry. But by the end of the 30s, nylon had been developed and nylon stockings replaced rayon ones.

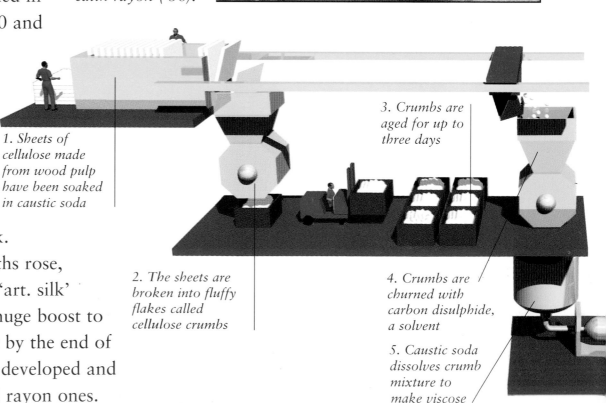

1. Sheets of cellulose made from wood pulp have been soaked in caustic soda

2. The sheets are broken into fluffy flakes called cellulose crumbs

3. Crumbs are aged for up to three days

4. Crumbs are churned with carbon disulphide, a solvent

5. Caustic soda dissolves crumb mixture to make viscose

NATTY KNITS

The 1920s saw a huge expansion of the knitting industry as knitwear became fashionable for outer garments instead of just being used for underwear and sportswear. Industrial knitting machines were used to produce enormous quantities either of flat or circular jersey materials that could be cut up into shapes and sewn together afterwards, or fully-fashioned garments shaped automatically on the machine.

A short-sleeved jumper of the mid-'30s: advances in knitting allowed for elaborate designs with contrasting ribbed panels.

Textile workers operate power knitting looms in Minneapolis, '36.

FANTASTIC ELASTIC

Another important development was the creation of elastic yarns. Improved methods of collecting natural rubber resulted in longer 'strands' that could be made into yarn. Lastex appeared on the market in 1931. This was a core of rubber with cotton, silk, wool or rayon wound round it. It spelt the beginning of a whole new era of stretchier, more comfortable clothes.

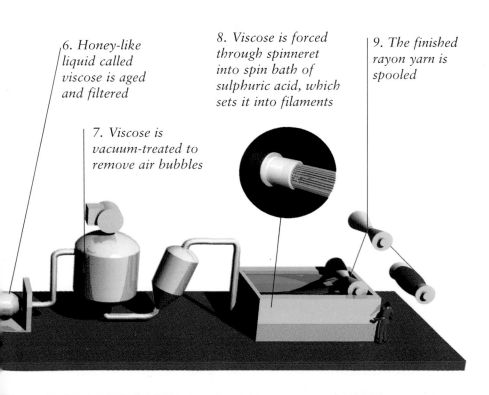

6. Honey-like liquid called viscose is aged and filtered

7. Viscose is vacuum-treated to remove air bubbles

8. Viscose is forced through spinneret into spin bath of sulphuric acid, which sets it into filaments

9. The finished rayon yarn is spooled

Elasticated waistbands meant that trousers could be held up without the need for braces.

GLOSSARY

ART DECO A decoration and art style based on geometric shapes and strong colours.

ART NOUVEAU A decoration and art style based on plant and flower motifs, and patterns of sinuous, curving lines.

BIAS CUT A way of cutting fabric diagonally which makes it fall into clinging folds.

BUSTLE A pad or framework worn under the back of a skirt.

COMMUNISM A political and social system which holds that private property should be abolished, and that instead it should be collectively owned and controlled by the people.

CREPE DE CHINE A thin, finely-wrinkled silk or rayon fabric.

CUBISM An art movement concerned with exploring abstract, geometric shapes.

DEPRESSION A period when there is a severe slump in business and industrial activity, and a rise in unemployment.

FASCISM A political movement or system, usually headed by a dictator, which suppresses democracy and enforces state control of all aspects of society.

FROCK COAT A long, waisted and almost knee-length coat.

FUTURISM An art movement concerned with the exploration of the energy and speed of machines.

LAMÉ A shiny fabric made by weaving metallic threads with silk, wool or other fibres.

LASTEX Trade name for an elastic yarn of rubber, plus silk, cotton or rayon.

MODERNISM The various experiments that took place in different art forms during the early decades of the twentieth century.

PLUS-FOURS Baggy trousers that end just below the knee.

PROHIBITION In the USA, the period 1920–33, when alcohol was banned by law.

RAYON An artificial, silk-like fabric made from wood pulp or chips.

SPAT A cloth or leather shoe covering usually fastened under the instep with a strap.

TAMBOUR Embroidery done on a tambour frame of two hoops that keep the fabric taut.

FASHION HIGHLIGHTS

- First elasticized bathing suit, by Jantzen — 19
- 'Chanel No 5' perfume launched — 19
- Duke of Windsor starts Fair Isle trend — 19
- Edith Head begins work in Hollywood — 19
- Patou puts monogram on his clothing — 19
- Adrian begins working in Hollywood — 19
- 19
- Patou brings out first suntan oil — 19
- 19
- Schiaparelli's first full collection — 19
- Mainbocher opens salon in Paris — 19
- 19
- 19
- Alice Marble wears shorts at Wimbledon — 19
- Lelong's 'editions' (ready-to-wear) launched — 19
- Schiaparelli uses zip as design statement — 19
- 19
- 19
- Polaroid sunglasses invented — 19
- Schiaparelli: 'Snuff', first perfume for men — 19

30

TIMELINE

	WORLD EVENTS	TECHNOLOGY	FAMOUS PEOPLE	ART & MEDIA
20	•USA: women get vote; Prohibition begins (to '33)	•Hairdryer first made	•Joan of Arc canonized	•D.H. Lawrence: Women in Love
21	•Chinese communist party founded	•Insulin discovered	•Marie Stopes opens Britain's first birth control clinic	•Rudolph Valentino stars in The Sheik
22	•Russia becomes USSR	•Choc-ice (Eskimo pie) invented	•Tutankhamen's tomb opened •Gandhi jailed (to '24)	•James Joyce: Ulysses •T.S. Eliot: The Wasteland
23	•Italy: Mussolini seizes power	•Autogiro (early helicopter) flown in Spain		•Cecil B. de Mille The Ten Commandments
24	•Britain: first Labour government elected	•First motorway opens, in Italy	•Death of Lenin	•Gershwin: Rhapsody in Blue
25		•Scotch tape invented	•George Bernard Shaw wins Nobel Prize for Literature	•F. Scott Fitzgerald: The Great Gatsby
26	•Britain: General Strike •Mussolini's dictatorship	•JL Baird: first television •Godard: first rocket	•Gertrude Ederle swims the Channel •Valentino dies	•Fritz Lang: Metropolis
27	•German stock market collapses	•First Volvo car made •Polyesters first used	•Charles Lindbergh is first to fly the Atlantic solo	•First successful 'talkie', The Jazz Singer
28	•USSR: Stalin's first five-year plan	•Discovery of penicillin •Electric razor patented	•Death of Emeline Pankhurst	•Disney: First Mickey Mouse cartoon
29	•USA: Wall Street Crash		•Hoover elected president of USA	•Mondrian: Composition in a Square
30	•India: Gandhi leads Salt March protest	•Planet Pluto identified	•Amy Johnson is first woman to fly to Australia	•Chrysler Building completed •Dietrich in The Blue Angel
31	•Japanese army occupies Chinese Manchuria	•Lastex yarn introduced	•Al Capone arrested for tax fraud	•Dali: Limp Watches •Cagney in The Public Enemy
32	•Nazis take control of Reichstag (parliament)	•Polythene created •First radio telescope	•Amelia Earhart flies solo across the Atlantic	•Carwardine's 'Anglepoise' lamp
33	•Hitler in power, as Chancellor of Germany	•Lemaître proposes Big Bang theory		•Fay Wray in King Kong •Garbo in Queen Christina
34	•China: Communists led by Mao on Long March	•Nylon invented •Cat's-eye road studs first used	•Shirley Temple wins an Oscar aged six	
35	•Italy invades Abyssinia (Ethiopia)	•First TV broadcasting station built, in Germany	•Malcolm Campbell sets 300 mph land speed record	•Fred Astaire & Ginger Rogers in Top Hat
36	•Spanish Civil War begins •Edward VIII abdicates	•Volkswagen Beetle designed by Porsche	•Jessie Owens stars at Berlin Olympics	•Frank Lloyd Wright: Falling Water
37	•India: Congress Party wins elections	•Ballpoint pen invented •Polyurethanes discovered		•Picasso: Guernica •Disney: Snow White
38	•Germany & Austria unite (Anschluss)	•Teflon discovered		
39	•Spanish Civil War ends •World War II begins	•Heinkel built first jet aircraft	•Sigmund Freud dies	•Selznick: Gone With the Wind •Garland in The Wizard of Oz

INDEX

012445